LIFE CYCLES

Text by Marco Ferrari

Illustrations by Ivan Stalio

RSVP

RAINTREE
STECK-VAUGHN
PUBLISHERS
A Steck-Vaughn Company

Austin, Texas

Published by Raintree Steck-Vaughn Publishers, an imprint
of Steck-Vaughn Company

Consultant: Gregory Haenel, Ph. D., Rutgers University
Editor: Kathy DeVico
Electronic Production: Lyda Guz, Scott Melcer
Project Manager: Joyce Spicer

Library of Congress Cataloging-in-Publication Data
Ferrari, Marco, 1954–
    Life cycles/text by Marco Ferrari; illustrated by
Ivan Stalio.
        p.   cm — (Everyday life of animals)
    Includes bibliographical references and index.
    Summary: Discusses the stages of life for different
types of animals, from mating and birth through raising
the young and living in various environments and groups.
    ISBN 0-8172-4197-3
    1. Animals—Juvenile literature. 2. Animal life cycles—
Juvenile literature. [1. Animal life cycles. 2. Animals—
Habits and behavior.] I. Stalio, Ivan, ill. II. Title.
QL49.F448   1999
591.56 — dc21   98-9268
                                                    CIP
                                                    AC

Printed in Italy
Bound in the United States

1 2 3 4 5 6 7 8 9 0   02 01 00 99 98

Photo credits [and Acknowledgements] that appear on page 64
constitute an extension of this copyright page.

Contents

Introduction 5

Lifestyles 6

Life Begins 8

Phases of Growth 10

Metamorphosis 12

Nests and Eggs 14

Parents 16

Early Days 18

First Food 20

Growing Up 22

Learning 24

Males and Females 26

Rivalry 28

Communication 30

Songs and Croaks 32

Relationships 34

Groups of Females 36

Hierarchies 38

Loners 40

Territory 42

Mating Grounds 44

Courtship 46

Mating 48

Living in Groups 50

Colonies 52

Flocking 54

Societies 56

Cooperation 58

Glossary 60

Index 63

Further Reading 64

Acknowledgments 64

An adult African elephant

Introduction

Blue-footed boobies during courtship

Millions of plants and animals struggle for survival every day of their lives. Each of them uses countless strategies in an effort to win the battle of life. Some depend on cunning, some on speed, some on strength or on **mimicry** to ensure their genes will be passed on to the next generation. A lion chasing a zebra is a classic example of what 19th-century scientists defined as "the struggle for life." The predator has to be faster and more cunning than its prey, while the prey depends largely on the principle of safety in numbers. But animals have invented much more subtle ways of ensuring their survival. Every strategy, every move and step made by most species can be explained by the one thing every individual is aiming for: reproduction. The goal is to contribute with as many genes as possible to future generations. Every animal and every plant has adopted a different lifestyle that is successful within its specific environment. Some simple life forms depend on the effective strategy of number. Bacteria, for example, literally overrun their environment with millions of tiny copies of themselves. More complex organisms produce fewer offspring as a rule, but a lot more energy goes into ensuring their survival, and mates are selected more carefully. This is what lies behind the incredible acrobatics of the male bird of paradise as he displays his plumage to the female, or extraordinary structures such as the peacock's tail or the male deer's antlers, which have the sole purpose of convincing the female that the owner is the most desirable male and that she should mate with him. It is also what lies behind the territorial struggles, sometimes battles to the death, which become more and more ritualized as animals **evolve**. But it is in the care of their offspring that some of the highest degrees of perfection in **adaptation** to the surrounding world have been achieved. **Mammals** devote much of their body resources to raising their young. Some insects even sacrifice themselves by allowing their **larvae** to feed on their internal organs. *Life Cycles* looks at the strategies animals have developed, their complex interactions with other members of the same species, and the extraordinary solutions adopted in their struggle for survival.

Lifestyles

Animals appear to face many choices. Live alone, or in a society? Lay many eggs, or only a few? Be choosy in seeking a mate, or leave it up to chance? Each of these alternatives involves a different complex life cycle, either rich and fascinating, or simple but effective.

Various mechanisms are involved in making these choices. They can be understood only when seen as part of the theory of evolution by means of natural selection, which was formulated in the 19th century by the English naturalist Charles Darwin. Every characteristic of an animal, said Darwin, evolved solely to allow the individual to transmit its genetic makeup to its descendants. Behavior can be explained in the same way. The long history of the evolution of life on Earth has molded behavior to make possible the survival and reproduction of the species. The modern theory of evolutionary biology, which developed in the 1960s, went on to explain more in detail other phenomena, which formerly seemed incomprehensible, such as animal societies and the "sacrifice" of the worker bees and the ants, who delegate reproduction to the queen alone.

When we say that an animal is faced with a choice, this does not mean that the decision is a conscious one, but only that billions of years of behavioral evolution make the individual behave as if it possessed a knowledge about its future. It is only from this point of view, of dateless time and extremely slow changes, that we can understand how animals behave and why animals behave as they do.

SOCIAL LIFE
The social life of many mammals, like these Thomson gazelles, is often governed by precise rules, which va according to the season and the environment. For example, to defend themselves from predators, the gazelles gather in groups to discourage and confuse the attacker by their number. But when it is time to give birth, they look for a peaceful, private place.

GROWING A NEW LIMB
Starfish are marine **invertebrates**. There are about 1,800 species living in oceans throughout the world. Most starfish have five hollow arms covered with short spines and tiny pincers. If an arm is bitten off, the starfish can grow a new one in its place. The majority of starfish reproduce by laying eggs that hatch into new individuals, but a few species of starfish reproduce by dividing their bodies in two pieces. Each part becomes a new individual.

BREAKING OUT AT BIRTH
Like most modern **reptiles**, crocodiles lay eggs from which their offspring hatch after a period of **incubation**. This young crocodile is pulling itself out of its egg. The tiny crocodile has a special patch on its snout to help break through the egg's leathery covering.

ANIMALS THAT LOOK LIKE FLOWERS
Although they look like plants, sea anemones are invertebrate marine animals. They attach themselves to hard surfaces, such as a rock or seashell, and seldom move. These anemones are competing for space.

PRIVATE NESTING HABITS
The female hornbill seals herself inside a cavity in a tree, rock face, or earth bank when nesting. She relies on the male to bring food and water, which he passes through the nest hole. She stays there until her chicks are half-grown.

Life Begins

Animals reproduce in a variety of ways. Only a small number of species (about 3 percent) give birth to live young. They are usually land animals, the offspring of which must be well developed when they are born in order to survive. The majority of animals lay eggs, from which their young emerge after a period of incubation. Most animals reproduce sexually; the sperm and egg from the two parents combine to form a new individual, with a mixture of chromosomes from both. A few animals, such as the sponge, can also reproduce **asexually**, which means that a new individual is formed from a single parent.

NESTING IN A HOLE IN THE GROUND
Many snails, including the common garden snail, dig holes in soft, damp soil where they place their eggs. They cover the eggs with earth to keep them safe from predators until they hatch. After a few weeks, tiny, fully formed snails emerge.

CORAL REPRODUCTION
Coral reefs are made up of millions of tiny, soft-bodied animals, called polyps. When breeding, the polyps release bundles of eggs and sperm that float upward and burst open. The sperm and eggs combine to form larvae, which drift in the ocean until they settle and turn into polyps themselves.

Live births

The Arabian oryx is a species of antelope that lives in the deserts of Arabia and Iraq. Like almost all mammals, it gives birth to live young. The female oryx usually produces a single calf; multiple births are rare. The baby oryx is on its feet a few minutes after birth and can keep up with the rest of the herd within a few hours.

Asexual reproduction

Up until the 19th century, sponges were thought to be plants. Today biologists class them as animals. Some sponges reproduce asexually in a process called **budding**. This occurs when a piece of the adult animal separates and becomes a new individual. Many sponges also reproduce sexually.

The final molt

Cicada **nymphs** live underground for several years. They **molt** five times before emerging as fully formed adults.

Developing outside mother's body

The female dogfish attaches a sac containing her embryo to a piece of seaweed. The **embryo** stays there for 6 to 9 months before hatching. The young dogfish shown below is emerging from its sac to begin adult life.

Phases of Growth

Many plants reproduce asexually, but most often it is invertebrates that do so. Almost all **vertebrates** (mammals, fish, reptiles, birds, and **amphibians**) reproduce sexually. In sexual reproduction, two sex cells (sperm and egg), each carrying half the number of chromosomes typical of the species, combine in a process called **fertilization**. The fertilized egg is called an embryo. Fertilization and the development of the embryo can occur inside or outside the female parent, depending on the species. The embryo develops and grows until it is ready for hatching or birth. Many animals, such as frogs, go through another stage of development before they reach their adult form.

FROM EGG TO LARVA TO ADULT
Gastropods (snails and slugs) live on land, in freshwater, and in the ocean. Some species, like the Portuguese orange sea snail shown here, lay strings of eggs in tide pools along rocky shorelines. The fertilized eggs hatch into larvae, called **veligers**, which can swim. The veligers then drift to the bottom of the pool, where they turn into crawling snails.

A FERTILIZED EGG
The small red spot in the middle of this egg yolk is a 3-day-old chicken embryo. One week later, the tiny embryo will be shaped like a chick.

FROM EGG TO CHICKEN
After about a month, the chick is fully formed and covered in soft **down**. It uses its beak to break the eggshell and hatches. The chick continues to grow until it becomes an adult, but it does not pass through another stage of development.

FROM EGG TO TADPOLE

During the breeding season, many frogs gather together in large, noisy groups. The females respond to loud mating calls made by the males. Very few frogs give birth to live young; most lay eggs in or near water. The female produces anywhere between 1 and 25,000 eggs, depending on the species. In most species, the eggs are fertilized outside the frog's body and are left to hatch by themselves. Only a few species protect and care for their eggs and young. Inside the egg a tiny tadpole with a round body and a long tail develops. When the tadpole hatches, it lives in the water and breathes through gills, like a fish.

FROM TADPOLE TO FROG

Unlike adult frogs, tadpoles are mainly **herbivores**. They feed on algae and other underwater plants. After a period of growth, the tadpole undergoes a striking change. Its tail gradually shrinks away, and hind- and forelimbs appear. It also develops jaws, lungs, eyelids, and a new digestive system to cope with a mainly **carnivorous** diet as an adult. This process is called **metamorphosis**.

North American leopard frog

■ MORE ABOUT   FROGS AND TOADS

Frogs and toads belong to the same group of tailless amphibians, called Anura. It is not wrong to refer to both as "frogs," although they have differences in appearance and lifestyle. Generally speaking, frogs live in or near water, have longer limbs and a smoother skin, while toads live in damp places away from water, are rounder, and have more warty skins. There are about 3,500 species of frogs and toads. They have successfully colonized every continent except for Antarctica, although the greatest variety (about 80 percent of all species) inhabit tropical and subtropical regions. They live in many habitats, from deserts, mountains, and savannas, to tropical rain forests.

Metamorphosis

As we have already seen, most kinds of frogs go through major changes as they grow: egg—tadpole—frog. The majority of invertebrates also pass through a juvenile, or larval stage. The most striking changes occur in certain types of insects, such as butterflies and moths, beetles, flies, and wasps. Their life cycles have four stages: egg—larva—**pupa**—adult. The larva differs greatly from the adult. It is wingless, and its lifestyle is suited for growth and development rather than for reproduction. The larva usually lives in a different habitat from the adult and eats different kinds of food. This ensures that members of the same species do not compete for space and food. The larva becomes a pupa and then an adult.

AMAZING INSECTS!

Of all the animals that have been described scientifically, the class Insecta contains the largest number of species. About five-sixths of all animals are insects. Furthermore, although nearly one million species of insects are known, scientists estimate that there are at least two million more species that have yet to be discovered.

A caterpillar hatches from its egg.

■ MORE ABOUT BUTTERFLIES AND MOTHS

Butterflies and moths belong to a huge order of insects, called **Lepidoptera**. The name is Greek and means "scaly winged." It refers to the dusty scales that cover the wings, bodies, and legs of moths and butterflies. Although they belong to the same order, moths and butterflies differ in size and lifestyle. Most moths are nocturnal (active at night), whereas butterflies are diurnal (active during the day). Moths usually have larger bodies, smaller wings, and are a duller color than butterflies. Not only do butterflies have more brightly colored wings, but they also hold them vertically over their backs when resting, which creates a delightful display. Moths generally fold their wings when at rest. There are over 100,000 species of moths and butterflies, and they live on every continent except for Antarctica. Almost all feed on plants, but some larvae feed on food crops and wool, silk, or fur clothing.

INSECTS AND EGGS

Almost all insects reproduce sexually. The females lay eggs. Many have a long tube, called an **ovipositor**, which they use to place their eggs where they want them. While baby insects are inside the egg, they feed on liquid yolk. When they are fully developed, the young insects hatch. Some bite their way out of the egg. Others simply grow until they burst out of the egg.

1

Metamorphosis of the swallow-tail butterfly

2. The caterpillar turns into a pupa (chrysalis). It builds a protective cocoon.

3. The chrysalis changes into an adult, splits the cocoon, and a butterfly (imago) emerges. The four stages in the life cycle of a butterfly, and other insects like it, are known as complete metamorphosis.

2

1. A caterpillar has a pair of **antennae** and a cluster of tiny eyes on each side of its head. Caterpillars have no wings and many legs.

3

4. A fully developed butterfly

4

Nests and Eggs

Some animals lay their eggs in the ocean or in freshwater and leave them to hatch and grow up on their own. These animals usually lay a large number of eggs, since many eggs and youngsters will be eaten by predators. Other parents spend a large amount of time and effort caring for their young. Preparing a home, whether it be a nest, den, or simply a well-chosen spot for egg-laying or birth, often requires planning and lengthy preparation. An ideal home needs to offer protection from the weather and safety from predators. Animals use many clever methods to prepare for the arrival of their young.

HEAT-REGULATED INCUBATORS

The mallee fowl of southern Australia is a member of the **megapode** family. The male bird spends many months of the year working on the nest. First he digs a hole and fills it with leaves and grass. Then he covers it with sandy soil to make a mound, and hollows out chambers inside where the female lays her eggs. The decaying vegetation below creates heat to incubate the eggs without further help from the parents. Mallee fowls are thought to mate for life, and many pairs use the same nest year after year.

■ MORE ABOUT MEGAPODES

Megapodes are a family of 12 species of game birds that live in rain forests, beach vegetation, and scrub in Australia, Southeast Asia, and on some Pacific Islands. Most species nest in mounds or holes in the ground.

A FATHER'S CARE

The female Iberian midwife toad lays a string of 20 to 60 eggs. After fertilizing them, the male toad winds the sticky string of eggs around his waist and hind legs. He carries the eggs around with him on land, keeping them safe from predators. After about a month, when the eggs are ready to hatch, he moves to the water, where the eggs break open, and tiny tadpoles emerge.

HANGING BASKETS

The lesser-masked weaverbird builds a hanging nest using grass and twigs. The male builds the nest to attract a female. When he has finished weaving the nest, he hangs beneath it, flapping his wings and trying to catch the attention of females. Once a female accepts the nest, she lines the inside with soft grass and feathers and lays her eggs. The nest hanging far above the ground keeps the eggs and chicks safe from snakes and other predators.

COLOR CHANGES

At breeding time the tiny male three-spined stickleback fish turns bright red and blue as he sets about building a nest to attract a female. Using strands of water plants and secretions from his kidneys to stick them together, he builds a spherical nest. When a female shows interest, he shows her the nest, and if she approves, she lays her eggs inside. The male fertilizes the eggs and protects them until they hatch. As he cares for the eggs, his skin turns to more neutral colors so that he will not attract predators.

Parents

After weeks, months, or in some cases, even years of preparation, the animal babies are finally born. During the first weeks of life, the two main chores for parents are keeping their often helpless offspring safe from predators, and finding enough food for them to survive. In many cases, care of the newborn animals is left almost entirely to the mother. Among mammals, the female feeds her young on milk that she produces. Mammal mothers usually lick their offspring clean soon after birth to clear their skins (particularly the nostrils) of fetal membrane. The mother can then recognize her newborn by its scent. Among birds, males often help their mates feed and care for offspring. In only a few species, such as the sea horse, are the fathers entirely responsible for the young.

■ MORE ABOUT THE PLATYPUS
Almost all mammals give birth to live young. However, the unique duck-billed platypus of eastern Australia and Tasmania is one of only three species of egg-laying mammals. (The other two are species of echidnas, which live in Australia or New Guinea.) The platypus spends most of its life in freshwater lakes and streams, where it feeds on fish, frogs, **crustaceans**, mollusks, tadpoles, and earthworms. It is an excellent swimmer, using its sensitive beak to find food and navigate underwater. The platypus is one of the very few mammals with venom. The male has a poison spur on the ankle of each hind foot, which it uses to fight with other males during the mating season. A jab from the spur contains enough poison to kill a dog.

AN EGG-LAYING MAMMAL
The female platypus digs a long, twisting passage in the earth with a burrow at the end. There she lays between one and three sticky, soft-skinned eggs about 2 weeks after mating. She curls her body around the eggs, and after about 10 days of incubation, they hatch. The platypus nurses her young for about 4 months. Since she has no nipples, her babies have special long lips to drink the milk as it oozes from pores under her fur. The young platypuses stay in the burrow for about 4 months. During that time, when the mother leaves the burrow to hunt, she plugs the entrance with soil to keep out predators.

KEEPING SAFE IN FATHER'S POUCH
The female sea horse lays several thousand eggs into a special pouch on the male's abdomen. The male fertilizes the eggs, feeds them with a nourishing liquid that the pouch secretes, and keeps them safe from predators. After a few weeks, a **brood** of sea horses hatches; the young are pushed out from the pouch by a series of contractions.

CARRYNG WATER TO THIRSTY CHICKS
Most species of sandgrouse live in dry regions of Africa and the Middle East. Their young usually hatch in nests that are far from watering holes. For at least 2 months, until they are old enough to fly, the babies rely on their father to bring them drinking water. The male sandgrouse flies to the watering hole, which is sometimes 12 to 20 miles (20 to 30 km) away, and soaks his specially adapted and absorbent breast feathers in the water. He stays in the water for up to 20 minutes, soaking up liquid. Then, with his precious cargo onboard, he flies back to the nest. When he returns he stands up straight, and the young birds run to drink from his breast. When they have drunk their fill, he rubs his belly in the sand to dry his feathers. Although female birds are capable of carrying water, and will do so if the male dies, the job is generally done by males. By dividing the work involved in caring for their young, the parents are more likely to be able to raise their brood to adulthood.

MAKING CONTACT AFTER BIRTH
The massive female bison of North America usually gives birth to a single calf after about 9 months' **gestation**. The female often leaves the herd to give birth, rejoining it as soon as her calf is strong enough to stand up. Immediately after birth she licks her baby clean, freeing its nostrils so that is can breathe, and drying its fur so that its tiny body can hold in more heat. This act of motherly care establishes a bond that lasts for about 3 to 4 years.

Early Days

As the young animals grow, parents spend time and energy protecting them from predators. Even normally calm animal parents, especially females, become aggressive and will sometimes place themselves in danger when defending their offspring. Many mothers carry their young on their backs during the first weeks or months of life. This allows them to move more quickly than they could if the young were following on their own and also saves the babies precious energy needed for growth. In many vertebrate animals, particularly mammals, affectionate and long-lasting relationships are established.

HITCHING A RIDE
When danger threatens, female swans ferry their brood out of harm's way. The cygnets nestle into the feathers on their mother's back. Swans can be very aggressive when defending their young.

■ **MORE ABOUT SCORPIONS**
There are over 1,200 species of scorpions. They all have long, venomous tail stings and six pairs of legs with pincers. Scorpions are mainly nocturnal and feed on spiders and insects. They use the front pair of pincers for grasping prey and tearing it apart. During courtship scorpions perform a ritual dance during which the male fertilizes the female. Males that stay near females after mating are sometimes killed and eaten by them. The fertilized eggs develop inside the female and, several months after mating, live young are born. A typical litter has from 6 to 90 young scorpions.

IN THE SHELTER OF A LETHAL STING
Newborn scorpions crawl onto their mother's back, where they are protected from predators by her sting. They stay on her back for one week or longer. During that time they absorb water through the female's skin and use food reserves built up before birth. If the female scorpion is unable to spend a lot of time caring for her young, they will not survive.

TAKING CARE OF BABY

Chimpanzees are social animals and live in small bands, usually based on family relationships. These small bands often group together in communities of up to 100 individuals. Female chimpanzees can give birth at any time of year to a single baby (or, more rarely, twins) after 8 to 9 months of gestation. Mother chimpanzees nurse their young for as long as 2 or 3 years. During this time, very strong relationships develop between the mother and her offspring. This special relationship appears to last throughout the animals' lifetimes, even after the birth of other offspring. If a female dies while caring for a young chimpanzee, its older brothers and sisters will often take care of it. Chimpanzees use a wide range of sounds and facial expressions. They often kiss, hug, embrace, and groom one another, seeming to show affection and care for each other within the group.

A female chimpanzee carefully removes something from her young's eye.

BUILDING FAMILY BONDS

After a gestation period of about 3 months, female cheetahs give birth to 2 to 4 cubs. Because the cubs are born blind and helpless, the mother cheetah gives birth in thick scrub or dense bush, where her cubs will be safe from predators. Juveniles have a thick mane on their necks and shoulders, which acts as **camouflage**. It makes them look larger and fiercer than they actually are, and gives the mother something to grip onto when carrying them by the scruff of the neck. Cheetahs nurse their young for about 3 months, although by 6 weeks the cubs are big enough to begin to learn how to hunt. Like all members of the cat family, cheetahs keep very clean. The mother cheetah spends time grooming her cubs. They are independent by about 18 months of age.

First Food

A plentiful supply of high-quality food is essential during the early stages of an animal's life. Protein, vitamins, sugars, and fats are needed to help the young animal develop and grow. Those parents that are not involved in caring for their young often lay their eggs on or near a rich food source, so that their offspring will have food at hand when they hatch. Mammal babies are among the most fortunate of young animals, because their mothers nurse them until they can feed themselves. During the first few days after birth, the mother's milk also contains antibodies to protect the baby from infection. Bird parents are kept busy for weeks after their chicks hatch.

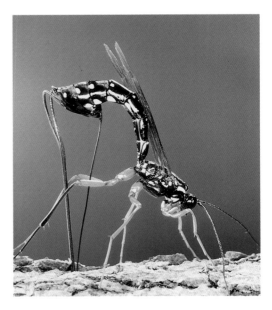

PREPARING MEALS IN ADVANCE
Many insects lay their eggs directly on or in food sources, so that when the larvae hatch they will have a ready supply of food. The larva of the ichneumon wasp shown here feeds on the larvae of wood wasps that develop in pine trees. The female ichneumon wasp searches the bark of trees until she detects a larva underneath. Using a long, specially adapted tube, she bores a hole in the trees and places an egg on top of the wood wasp larva. When the ichneumon wasp larva hatches, it eats the larva of the wood wasp before turning into a pupa. The pupa develops in the safety of the tree until it becomes an adult wasp the following year.

TAP THE RED SPOT FOR FOOD
Like most species of gulls, herring gulls mate for life. In the early summer, the birds gather in colonies to nest on cliff ledges or coastal islands. After mating, the female lays two or three eggs. Parents share the task of incubating the eggs, switching every few hours. When the chicks hatch, they know by instinct to peck at the red spot on their mother's bill. This makes her **regurgitate** the food she has in her crop. The chicks stay close to the nest for about a week. Their parents protect them from other adults, which sometimes prey on their neighbors' young.

CROP MILK FOR HUNGRY CHICKS
Two groups of birds, flamingos and pigeons, feed their young on crop milk. Since flamingos usually nest far from food sources, they solve the problem of carrying food back to their young by regurgitating a kind of "milk" or "soup" made from food they have swallowed themselves, called crop milk. Both male and female birds produce crop milk. Studies have shown that even flamingos that are not parents care for orphan chicks in this way. The persistent begging calls of the hungry youngsters seem to stimulate the production of a hormone that allows the birds to produce milk.

AQUATIC MAMMAL BABIES
A Galápagos sea lion mother nurses her pup. **Aquatic** mammals, including whales, dolphins, seals, and walruses, all feed their young on milk.

A flamingo parent feeding its chick crop milk. The baby birds lose their fluffy down at about 12 weeks. It takes several years for their gray juvenile color to change to adult pink.

■ MORE ABOUT FLAMINGOS
Flamingos are strange-looking birds, with very long legs and necks, small heads, and huge, curved beaks. They have large bodies and white or pink feathers, depending on the species and their diet. Males are 32 to 57 inches (80 to 145 cm) tall, while females are slightly shorter. There are several species, and they range over southern South America, Southern Africa, North Africa, southern Europe, and the Middle East. They are social birds and stay together in flocks. At mating time they come together in huge **colonies**. An estimated 2 million birds gather in a single colony around Lake Nakuru in the Rift Valley, Kenya. Flamingos mate for life, and both parents help build the nest of mud where the female lays a single egg. The parents take turns incubating the egg until it hatches, and both share in the tasks of raising their offspring. Flamingos seem to live quite a long time; 50-year-old birds have been recorded in the wild. Flamingos are wading birds. When feeding, they hold their bills upside down in the water or mud, straining it for algae, mollusks, fish, or small invertebrates.

Growing Up

The age at which the young become capable of surviving alone varies greatly from species to species. A few days or even less may be sufficient. All invertebrates, insects, and many fish or reptiles, for example, are independent as soon as they are born, or at most a few days after birth. Most of the abilities for survival are instinct, and the offspring have little to learn from their parents. They are able to find food for themselves immediately. But if the baby has to develop complex skills, such as learning how to hunt, for example, or how to move around in the forest canopy and not fall from trees, then it is dependent on its parents for much longer. The animals that take the longest to become independent are those with the largest brains, such as birds or mammals.

ORANGUTAN
The offspring of the orangutan, an ape that lives in Southeast Asia, stay with their mother a long time, because they have to learn to choose the right fruits and leaves to eat, and how to move about the forest. The young monkeys also learn to build shelters in the trees, where they can rest at night. The newborn babies are able only to hold on to their mother's fur for protection, especially from male members of the group. The males are dangerous, because they are always looking for females to mate with, and will chase away the baby if it is in the way.

KANGAROO
Marsupials, or pouched animals, such as this small kangaroo, have developed a unique method of developing the embryo. The **neonate**, or undeveloped baby, slowly moves from the uterus to the mother's marsupial pouch, where it latches onto her nipple. Not until many weeks later does the birth take place, when the baby kangaroo is ready to leave the pouch for the first time. It follows its mother as she moves around in search of fresh grass to eat.

ELEPHANT SOCIETY
Within elephant herds, both Indian (shown left) and African, different kinds of social behaviors are found, both friendly and aggressive. The relationships between the elephants change over time. This is why elephant calves can take up to 6 or 7 years to grow up. They only become adult members of the group once they have learned all the rules of elephant behavior. They stay with their mother until they are fully grown.

GOLDEN EAGLE
Eagles and many other birds of prey generally lay two eggs at different times. This is why the second chick to hatch is smaller. Often the older chick bullies or even kills the second chick. Then the parents can devote themselves to teaching their single offspring the art of hunting in flight.

■ MORE ABOUT GOLDEN EAGLES
Golden eagles start to breed when they are about 4 years old and keep the same mate for life. Each pair guards a territory and builds a nest, called an aerie. Many golden eagles build two nests and use them in alternate years, adding new material each time. Over the years, the shaggy nest might grow from 3 feet (1 m) to 10 feet (3 m) across.

Learning

Many young animals are taught by their parents to hunt and find food. Like all large cats, leopard cubs go with their parents on hunting trips. By watching them hunt and by practicing with their help, the cubs learn the skills they need to survive. Animals do not stop learning once they become adults. Many examples have been recorded where fully grown animals have discovered ways to find food or to improve its taste—often by accident. They have repeated the method later, and even taught it to other individuals in their group so that it becomes a part of their normal behavior.

■ MORE ABOUT MACAQUE MONKEYS

There are about 16 species in the Old World macaque monkey family. They live in Asia. Although color differs among the species, they are generally brown or blackish brown. Males are larger than females, weighing between 8 and 18 pounds (3.5 and 8 kg). Some species live along coastlines or on islands and are able to swim. They are omnivores, and they all have large cheek pouches in which they carry extra food. Japanese macaque monkeys live farther north than any other monkey. During the cold winters, they sometimes bathe in hot springs.

LEARNING FROM EACH OTHER
A young female Japanese macaque monkey on the Pacific island of Koshima learned that washing the sand from potatoes left by biologists made them taste better. After just a few weeks, the other monkeys in her troop began to do the same.

THE ENDLESS GAME OF LIFE

From early on in life, most young mammals play and have mock fights with their parents, brothers, and sisters. This helps them to develop control of their eyes and muscles, learning skills for defense and hunting that will be essential as adults. Through play animals that live in groups also learn about the group **hierarchy**, or "pecking order."

EGG-SMASHING TOOLS

Many animals have learned to use tools to find food, build homes, or frighten predators. Egyptian vultures like to eat ostrich eggs. The Egyptian vulture shown below is holding a stone in its beak, which it will smash down on the ostrich egg beneath. When they find eggs in sandy areas, where there are no suitable stones, the vultures sometimes fly quite long distances to find one.

MILK THIEVES

In Great Britain, where milk is still sometimes delivered to people's front doors, some titmice learned to pierce the bottle caps to get at the cream. The skill spread rapidly throughout the country as the titmice copied one another. Biologists think that the birds learned by watching each other, and the reward, a rich drop of cream, was enough to encourage them to try it themselves. Birds of different species have also been known to learn and copy others' behavior.

Males and Females

In some animal species, one sex is much larger or more striking in appearance than the other. This is called sexual **dimorphism**. In many species the males are larger, more aggressive, or more brightly colored than females of the same species. In some other species, such as anglerfish and spiders, the females are larger and more aggressive than the males. Biologists believe that these differences exist to help the species reproduce itself and survive. For example, if the female anglerfish were not huge and the males were not permanently attached to her, they would have trouble finding her in the dark ocean depths where they live, and it is unlikely that they would be able to reproduce.

> ### ■ MORE ABOUT ANGLERFISH
> There are over 200 species of anglerfish. Most of them live on the seabed, often in very deep waters. In many species the females have a long stalk on their back with a colored or luminous "bait" on the end. By waving this about, they attract fish that come close to investigate. When they are within range, the anglerfish swallows them.

A CLOSE RELATIONSHIP
Some female anglerfish grow twenty times larger than males. The male fish have pincerlike teeth and are unable to feed. During the breeding season, they bite into a female's skin and fertilize her eggs. They stay attached to her for the rest of their lives. The male is totally dependent on the female for food and oxygen; gradually, even his blood fuses with hers. Sometimes more than one male attaches himself to the same female.

A CAUTIOUS APPROACH
When a male spider wants to mate, he must be very careful to identify himself when approaching a female. Then he must make a quick escape afterward. Many females are larger than the males, and if they mistake the males for prey, they may eat them after mating. The eggs are laid in a silk sac that the female carries around with her or hides until the eggs hatch.

SIAMESE FIGHTING FISH
Siamese fighting fish, originally from Thailand, have been kept and bred for use in fighting contests. The specially bred fish are very brightly colored with long fins. The males are very aggressive; during courtship and mating, they bite and batter the females in a frenzied whirl of color. To attract the attention of the females, male fish can brighten or even change their colors.

MALE MAMMALS
Sexual dimorphism is common among mammals. The males are often larger and more powerful than the females. This is because the males fight among themselves; the biggest and strongest are the most successful, and they pass these characteristics on to their offspring. Females often mate with males that are in some way "superior" to the others. So the larger and more powerful males mate more often, and these characteristics are reproduced. The male sheep, or ram, is in the middle of this picture.

Rivalry

Animals not only have to defend themselves from predators of other species, but they also often have to struggle with members of their own species. During courtship and mating, males fight to gain or keep control of females or mating grounds. Some territorial animals defend their territory from others throughout the year. Social or herd animals often fight to establish or preserve their position within the group hierarchy. Young animals in a litter or clutch where food and warmth are scarce also compete with each other. Competition between sisters and brothers is called sibling rivalry.

KANGAROO BOXING
Kangaroos live in Australia, New Guinea, and New Zealand. The largest species, with males standing over 7 feet (2 m) tall, travel in groups led by a dominant male called the "old man" or "boomer." He dominates younger rivals by biting, kicking, and boxing.

INSECTS IN COMBAT
Sexual dimorphism, where males and females are quite different from each other, is common in insects. Among stag beetles, the males have greatly enlarged mandibles (jaws). They look like the antlers of a stag (male deer), hence the name of the species. The males use their huge jaws to wrestle with other males to compete for females. Rival stag beetles interlock their jaws in much the same way as stags do their antlers.

SIBLING RIVALRY
When food is scarce or the number of offspring is particularly large, brothers and sisters compete with each other for food. Among birds, the noisiest hatchlings with the largest gape attract their parents' attention and receive the most food.

■ **MORE ABOUT KOMODO DRAGONS**
Komodo dragons are the largest lizards in the world. They grow up to 10 feet (3 m) long and weigh about 300 pounds (135 kg). They are part of the monitor lizard family and live on Komodo Island and neighboring islands in Indonesia. The animals live in deep burrows where they lay eggs that hatch in April and May. The hatchlings live in trees during the first months of their lives. Although they feed mainly on **carrion**, adult Komodo dragons have been known to attack and eat members of their own species, as well as larger mammals, including humans.

A FEARSOME DISPLAY
Lizards often use threatening displays, including color changes, body inflation, push-ups, tail waving, and head movements to warn individuals of their own species or others to keep off their territory or away from a mate. Many males, like the Komodo dragons shown here, gain territory at the beginning of the mating season and defend it from others in ferocious battles.

Communication

Animals use a variety of signs and signals to communicate information to others. Some of the most common signals include: marking a territory with scent; showing a flash of color in defense or warning; singing or calling during courtship and mating, or to stay in touch; and body language for defense or for pulling rank.

SONG OF THE HUMPBACK WHALES

Whales have extremely good hearing. They can hear sounds called **phonations** that are far too high- or low-pitched for humans to hear. They can also tell from which direction sounds come. Humpback whales make a wide variety of sounds, strung together in a sequence that forms a "song" that lasts between 7 and 10 minutes and is then repeated. All the whales sing the same basic song, which they can hear from as far as 50 miles (80 km) away. So far scientists have been unable to determine what the songs mean, though they have discovered that the songs change as the whales mature.

■ MORE ABOUT HUMPBACK WHALES

The humpback whale is one of the largest whales. It is a baleen whale. **Baleen** is material that hangs in plates in the whale's mouth. These plates act as strainers to keep the **plankton** and small fish that the whale takes in with every mouthful of water. Similar to many other types of whales, humpbacks tend to graze (feed) in groups, or **pods**, of twenty or more animals. One of the most striking characteristics of the humpback whale is its white flippers, which it sometimes raises above the surface of the water. Humpback whales are also known for the long distances they travel—from the Arctic Circle to the warm waters of the Tropics, where they mate and give birth to their young.

MAY THE LOUDEST VOICE WIN

In the rutting (breeding) season each fall, stags hold roaring contests to compete for the possession of **harems** of up to 20 females. The males' voice boxes become enlarged during the rut. The loud, roaring bellows are an invitation to fight, although few animals ever come to blows, and most contests are settled by roaring alone. Roaring is an exhausting business; each stag bellows about 5 times per minute. The loudest animal wins.

LEARNING HUMAN LANGUAGE

Attempts to teach chimpanzees to speak have failed because they do not have the right voice boxes. Chimps taught to use sign language have learned to make short sentences and to recognize and express some concepts, such as "same" and "different." Their language skills are at a similar level to those of a 2- to 3-year-old child.

BODY LANGUAGE

Animals can express a wide range of emotions through the positions of parts of the body. Wolves communicate within the pack by the position of their tail and ears. Only the leader of the pack can keep its tail raised, for example, while all the others must keep their tails "humbly" lowered. When an animal wants to attack, it flattens its ears. This is how the wolf shows the others what it intends to do.

Songs and Croaks

The animal world is almost never silent; even in the depths of night, or in the middle of a desert, the calls of birds or cries of other animals can be heard. Most animals communicate using sound, because sound can cover large distances in a short amount of time. Animals use sound to attract members of the opposite sex, to keep away those of the same sex, to inform others of their presence, or to give warning. They produce sounds in many different ways. Some insects, such as crickets and grasshoppers, make sounds by rubbing their wings together; amphibians and mammals vibrate the vocal cords in their throats. Birds have a vocal organ near their lungs, called a **syrinx**. The syrinx contains many membranes that vibrate, so birds can produce a variety of different sounds.

FROG TALK
Tailless amphibians, including frogs and toads, are among the most skilled "singing" animals. Despite their small size, the males can make very loud noises. Most of them have large vocal sacs beneath their throats, which make their calls louder. The calls of the males can usually be heard during the brief mating season when they are used to attract females and keep away other males. Animals that prey on frogs know this, too. Guided by the sound, they lose no time in hurrying to the swamps where the "singers" are performing to swallow them whole.

■ MORE ABOUT AMPHIBIANS
About 370 million years ago, the amphibians were the first vertebrates to live on land. Nearly 4,000 species live on land today. There are the tailless amphibians, such as frogs and toads, those with tails, such as salamanders and newts, and a few species of strange limbless amphibians, called the caecilians. Most amphibians feed on insects and other small invertebrates they catch on the ground. All of them lay their eggs in a very humid environment or in water.

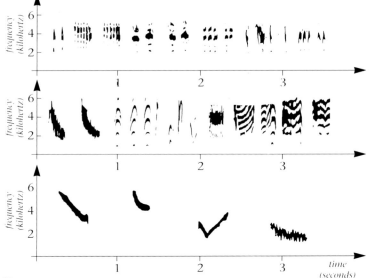

DIAGRAMS OF BIRD SONGS
Every bird has its own special song, which specialists study with highly sophisticated instruments. Above are some sonograms, which are diagrams of the songs of various species. They show the number of sounds made over a certain period of time. It has been shown that in some species the final song has to be learned from the parents, while other birds are born with all the songs in their brain.

GREAT REED WARBLER
Like many of the perching birds, the male great reed warbler sings in the spring to inform others of his presence. After he has marked out his territory and provided a quiet place for the female to lay her eggs, the male perches on a high cane and begins singing his shrill song. The song of the great reed warbler is one of the most characteristic sounds of the dense European marshes.

CHATTING BIRDS
Parrots (shown below) are among the most talkative in the world of birds. They can even do fairly good imitations of the human voice; often they say complete phrases. Mynah birds from Asia are even better mimics than parrots. Some succeed in learning more than 700 words, though they do not know their meanings.

Relationships

The basis of every group of animals, from the family to the most complex society, is the close relationship between the young and the female parent. It is the female that makes what scientists call the greatest "parental investment." She lays the eggs and, where parental care is involved, she is usually the one that protects and teaches the young. Few males take on family duties. Most are interested only in mating as often as possible. Only when the offspring are unable to survive alone, for example, because they need to learn to hunt or have to be fed with food that is hard to find, does the male lend a hand in raising them. Larger groups such as wolf packs, lion prides, and monkey societies are then formed, each with their own complex rules of social behavior.

THE GREAT ANTLERS OF THE MALE

Among the moose, and all those that belong to the deer family, it is the female that raises the young by herself. The male spends his time defending his territory and seeking females to mate with in that area. Moose have enormous antlers only so that males can fight with them. The rutting season is September to October. Young males use their antlers to challenge an older male, and also to violently shake trees and bushes to show other moose how strong they are. Moose pairs do not stay together very long. The dominant male follows a female around and keeps other males away until they have mated. Once they have mated and the calf is born, the pair splits up.

■ **MORE ABOUT HERONS**

The heron family consists of about sixty species. They live in all kinds of habitats around the world, except in the polar regions. Their long beaks and slender legs enable them to ambush their prey. Herons, egrets, and the black-crowned night heron wait patiently at the water's edge for fish, amphibians, or small mammals to come within reach of their stabbing beaks. Herons vary in color from the great white heron to the black African and Australian egrets, with a range of red, green, or brown plumage in between. A small group of herons, the bitterns, are well camouflaged against the thick canes, where they build their nests and lay their eggs. Most other herons nest close to each other in large colonies called heronries. Colonies are often mixed, with storks, spoonbills, and ibises sharing the space.

COMPLEX SOCIETIES

Baboons are among the monkeys most commonly found in the African savanna. Each group is an extended family, with a dominant male and a harem of females arranged in a hierarchy—order of dominance. But similar to human groups, baboon society changes all the time. The dominant male can be ousted by a younger male from another group, or the highest-ranking female can lose her place because of illness or fights. This is why young baboons have to learn their place in the group.

NESTS IN TREES

Herons and egrets build nests in trees to keep the eggs and chicks safe from predators. Even though they live side by side in a heronry, egrets are anything but friendly to their neighbors. A number of small territories are created within the heronry, off-limits to other members of the colony. If an adventurous chick leaves its nest, it is chased away and sometimes killed by its neighbors.

NOBODY BUT MOM

The bear family is very simple. It consists of the mother and her young. After mating, the male bear leaves the female to take care of the offspring by herself. The male becomes a complete stranger, and may even be a danger to the cubs. Bears are predators, and in the eyes of a male, a cub represents a chance to fill his stomach. The female must therefore not only be on the lookout for flooding rivers, wolves, or hunters, but also keep an eye on the males of her own species. The cubs stay with their mother for about three years.

Groups of Females

Both harems and **matriarchies** are groups of female animals living together. The difference between the two lies in the leadership. In harems, there is a dominant male, or group of males, to protect and control the females. Only the dominant male is allowed to mate with the females in the harem. Harems are common among mammals. Some harems are permanent, while others last only for the mating season. A matriarchy is a group of females led by a dominant female. Males are not allowed in the group and are only allowed to enter during the breeding season. They are sent away soon after mating. The females in a matriarchy care for and bring up their young together.

ELEPHANT SOCIETY
Family herds of elephants are led by a dominant grandmother elephant, or "matriarch." The herd she leads normally consists of her sisters, daughters, female cousins, and all their various offspring. As group leader, the matriarch is responsible for finding sufficient food and water, and for keeping the herd safe from predators and natural dangers. If, for example, a river must be forded, the matriarch will go first, finding the best route for the crossing. Within the herd, female elephants usually have their babies at about the same time. It is quite common for sister elephants, or mothers and daughters, to help each other by providing a baby-sitting service when a mother elephant needs a rest or wants to feed away from her baby.

STAG WITH HAREM
In the weeks leading up to the rut, male deer, called stags, become highly aggressive. They fight among themselves to gain control over the largest number of females. When mating is over, most species of deer split into single-sex groups of bachelor males, and females with their young, each with their own leaders. They remain in these groups until the next rut.

SEA LION HAREMS
Male sea lions are much larger than the females. During the breeding season, dominant males gather up to fifty females into harems. The males fight one another to win control over a piece of shoreline where the females will come ashore. When the females arrive at the breeding grounds, they give birth to a single pup conceived the year before and then mate again. They mate with the male that controls their area of shoreline.

■ MORE ABOUT COATIS
Coatis live in forests and scrublands in Central and South America. They are closely related to raccoons. Coatis have long, upturned snouts, which they use to probe for prey. They feed on insects and other invertebrates, birds, eggs, fruit, and small mammals. The males are solitary animals; they only join the female group during mating. Females build platforms in trees where they give birth to three to five young.

COOPERATIVE COATI GROUPS
Female coatis live together in cooperative groups of between 5 and 40 individuals. They share guard duties, engage in mutual grooming, and help each other raise young.

Hierarchies

The life of a pack, of a family, and of an animal society needs order. Each member of the group has to know precisely what its tasks, duties, and rights are. This is why hierarchies are formed within the pack. One male or female with special characteristics always emerges the winner from battles between the various members. The strongest, the smartest, or the most trustworthy takes command of the group, and has control over the other animals. The dominant figure often looks different and behaves differently from the other members of the group: it is larger, more colorful, and decides what to do at critical moments in the life of the pack.

FIGHTING FOR A MATE
Among horses, a single stallion dominates the rest of the herd, which is made up of females and colts. When still quite small, colts start to play at fighting, kicking each other, and rearing up on their hind legs. They are learning behavior that will be useful in adult life, and establishing a hierarchy. During the mating season, the stallion mates with all the females. He controls the herd until he is challenged and beaten by a younger male from a herd of "bachelors." Although he dominates his herd, a stallion does not have a large territory, just an area where grass and water are plentiful and through which the females have to pass. This social system is fairly rare in mammals; it is only found in two species of zebras, the Burchell, and mountain zebra, and a few other African species, such as the giant pig and the gelada baboon.

THE DOMINANT GRIFFON
The hierarchy among griffon vultures is created every time they feed, and it is temporary. When the griffons fling themselves on a carcass, the hungriest griffons are also the most aggressive. They try to chase away the other birds landing on the meat with open wings and extended claws. When they have eaten their fill, they become less aggressive, and other griffons take their place. This happens every time a vulture sights carrion. But if, as in Africa, there are different species of vultures present, the largest ones dominate, chasing away the others.

THE COLORS OF THE DOMINANT MALE
The social systems of baboons and mandrills are as different as the brilliant colors that distinguish them. The gelada baboons (below), for example, live in large colonies, usually of 50 to 250 animals, made up of small harems belonging to a single male, and groups of bachelor males. The harem is formed when a bachelor male succeeds in attracting one or more young females. Even though the males are dominant, it is the older and more experienced females who lead the group. The mandrills (right) live in the tropical forests of West Africa, and move in groups of about 20 animals under the command of a male. The brilliant colors of the gelada (bright red on their breasts, and purple lips) and the mandrills (blue and red cheeks) are displayed to show other members of the group when they want to mate, attack, or make peace.

Loners

The males and females of some animal species live by themselves for most of the year. They only meet with others of their species for a brief period during courtship and mating. They return to their solitary lives as soon as mating is over. When the offspring are born, the female takes care of them and brings them up on her own. In only a few cases, for example, among sea horses, do the males raise the young.

SOLITARY SALAMANDERS

Most salamanders live in temperate regions of the Northern Hemisphere. They live on land, in the water, or spend part of their time on land and part in the water, depending on the species. Salamanders meet at mating time and, after a brief courtship, mating takes place. In the more primitive salamanders, fertilization takes place outside the body. In some species, courtship is more elaborate, and fertilization occurs inside the female's body. The eggs are normally laid soon after mating, but sometimes the sperm is stored and egg-laying delayed.

LARGE GROUPERS

Groupers are large, heavy-bodied fish. Some species can grow to 7 feet (2 m) in length and weigh up to 500 pounds (225 kg). They live in warm waters throughout the world. Groupers tend to live in one place from which they hunt for prey. They are ferocious hunters.

ON ITS OWN

North American bison (also known as buffalo) are normally social animals. They were once numerous in North America (an estimated 50 million inhabited the Great Plains when Europeans arrived) and lived together in large herds. Numbers are now much reduced, and surviving animals live in herds of 20 to 40 individuals during most of their lives. However, in old age, they often wander off on their own, leaving the herd in preparation for death.

LONE HUNTERS

The lynx is a short-tailed member of the cat family. It lives in the forests of Europe, Asia, and northern North America. Most lynxes live alone in established territories, which they leave only during the mating season. During courtship, males make high-pitched wailing sounds, which females answer by howling. A litter of two or three kittens is raised by the mother. They stay with her until the next mating season, when they are chased away by new suitors.

THE SECRETIVE OCTOPUS

Octopuses are shy and secretive animals. They usually live by themselves in holes or crevices on the rocky seabed. At breeding time, one of the male's eight tentacles develops special adaptations. At first he uses it to caress his mate. Then he reaches inside his body and takes out packages of sperm, which he pushes into the female's body through her breathing tube.

Territory

We all feel comfortable in our own homes. We know where to go to find things, and we can keep out people we do not want to see. For the same reasons, many animals fight to establish a territory of their own, and they keep away rivals with various signals. Sounds, flashes of light, odors, movements of feathers, pincers, and claws are all used to mark a territory and defend it. There are different kinds of territories. The most common is a place where plenty of food is found. Hyenas, lions, wolves, and hummingbirds chase away others that come too close in order to defend an area where they know they will always be able to find food. Some animals defend a reproductive territory. Sea lions and elephant seals, for example, could certainly never catch fish on the beaches that they defend from outsiders. But the females with which the males will mate come ashore on just those stretches of beach. Frogs and many species of fish also construct their own reproductive territories.

CONCERTS IN THE JUNGLE
Howler monkeys are the largest monkeys in the South American rain forest. The males establish a vast territory, which they defend from other monkey bands by howls that can be heard as far as 3 miles (5 km) away. Each species has its own typical cry, which zoologists compare to the sound of a crowd in a football stadium. The howler monkey is able to make such loud cries because it has a specially adapted voice box.

SMALL UNDERWATER TERRITORIES
Many species of fish also defend a territory. Most territorial fish, such as the peacock blenny shown here, live in shallow coastal waters. The peacock blenny inhabits the rocky shorelines of the Mediterranean Sea. The male claims a small area of rocks and algae, and strongly defends it from other fish. He persuades females to lay their eggs in his territory. Knowing the area well means that the blenny can escape and hide from danger when necessary.

A QUIET LIFE

Sloths, which live in the tropical forests of Central and South America, are the last survivors of a long line of once-plentiful herbivores. These animals leave their tree only when they have to move to another tree or eliminate waste. When they do so, they dig a small hole in the ground at the base of the tree. It is thought that the excrement fertilizes the sloth's tree and at the same time keeps other sloths away with its odor. Sloths move far too slowly to ever fight battles, so all they have to do to protect their territory is mark it in this way.

HOMES IN THE SAND

Male fiddler crabs have a single huge claw that they move back and forth as though playing the violin. According to Charles Darwin, this evolved through males fighting each other for possession of females. Those with the biggest claws were the most successful at mating and passed the characteristic on to their offspring. The huge claw is also used to attract females to the holes in the sand where the males live. Thousands of these homes, each about 16 inches (40 cm) long, sometimes cover whole beaches; the crabs shelter in them when high tide comes or danger threatens.

■ MORE ABOUT FIDDLER CRABS

Fiddler crabs live on many tropical beaches. The crabs feed on the detritus (loose material) they find on the beach, such as the thin layer of bacteria and other small organisms that cover the sand. The crab puts a ball of sand in its mouth, swallows the nutritious parts, and leaves the rest in neat balls around its home. There are several species of fiddler crabs. When a number of different crabs live together on a beach, they divide the territory according to the sizes of their mouths. Those with large mouths live on the part where the grains of sand are large, while those with small mouths live in areas of fine sand.

Mating Grounds

A territory used only to attract females for mating is called a **lek**, or mating area. A bird lek is often an area of only a few square yards. It is a specific area in the prairies, savannas, or dense forests where males go to display themselves to females and let them select the best one. Some species, such as the American sage grouse, use the lek as a stage on which to display their beauty and strength. Other species, such as the bowerbirds of New Guinea and Australia, try to impress females by creating elaborate "gardens" quite unlike anything else in the animal kingdom. Very few mammals adopt the lek system, although male fallow deer have been known to use it under certain conditions. After mating, the task of raising the young falls to the females.

GARDENS MADE BY BIRDS
Bowerbirds live in New Guinea and Australia. At mating time, male bowerbirds try to impress females by building bowers—corridors or circles decorated with flowers, fruits, and feathers, often in striking colors. The females come to inspect the "gardens." They decide which is the best and choose its owner as their mate. The great gray bowerbird pictured below is building a decorated avenue. Other species make clean-swept courts, carpets of moss and fern, or decorate trees.

BATTLING FOR MATES

Topi (shown right) are a species of antelope. They are one of the few mammals to make use of the lek, although they only do so when the topi population is particularly dense. Generally the males occupy relatively small territories, and groups of females, which live separately, pass through them. But when the **population density** is high, the territories of the males shrink in size until they are no more than mating areas, from which the males try to attract females. Similar behavior occurs in the European fallow deer.

A STAGE SHOW IN THE PRAIRIE

The sage grouse lives in the North American prairie. During the mating season, the males place themselves in tiny territories within the mating area. There is a strict hierarchy. The larger and more experienced males occupy the center of the area, while the others take positions all around, with the lowest-ranking birds the farthest away. When the females arrive, the males begin their courtship dance: steps forward, wings rotated, stiff tail feathers raised, and white neck feathers puffed out into a frill. The females then choose the winner. Even though the males at the center of the area are chosen most often, those on the outside are not completely ignored.

KNIGHTS AND VASSALS

Ruffs are elegant wading birds that live in Europe. The dominant male, often those with the darkest ruffs (frills of feathers around their necks) position themselves at the center of the lek; the weaker males, with lighter ruffs, are around the edge. The dominant males try to gain favor with the females that pass by, showing themselves to be strong. The weaker males attempt to mate with the females on their way to the center. Since the females are initially attracted to the lek by the males with lighter ruffs, the dominant males do not mind them being there.

Courtship

During courtship animals try to attract mates in many different ways. Among birds, the male peacock shows off the splendid colors of his tail feathers, while the male of the common tern offers the gift of a fish to the chosen female. Others, like the great-crested grebe, perform ritual dances and exchange gifts. The male eagle calls a female with a loud, shrill cry. If she replies, these great birds of prey grip talons in midair, tumbling and cartwheeling across the sky.

A FISHY PROPOSAL
When the male tern wants to find a mate, he catches a fish and holds it in his beak until a female notices him. If she likes the fish, she will eat it. Then she waits to see how many more fish he will bring. If he turns out to be a good fisherman, she will accept his mating proposal, since she knows he will be a good provider for her chicks.

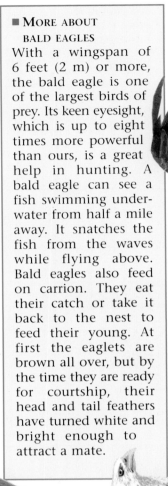

■ MORE ABOUT BALD EAGLES
With a wingspan of 6 feet (2 m) or more, the bald eagle is one of the largest birds of prey. Its keen eyesight, which is up to eight times more powerful than ours, is a great help in hunting. A bald eagle can see a fish swimming under-water from half a mile away. It snatches the fish from the waves while flying above. Bald eagles also feed on carrion. They eat their catch or take it back to the nest to feed their young. At first the eaglets are brown all over, but by the time they are ready for courtship, their head and tail feathers have turned white and bright enough to attract a mate.

46

THE DANCE OF THE GREBES
Great-crested grebes have an elaborate courtship dance, which lasts over a period of weeks. They start by shaking their heads at each other. If this goes well, they move on to the next stages, which include ritual **preening**, wing-spreading displays, diving, and the final "weed" dance, when the birds press against each other with pieces of weed in their beaks.

"LOOK AT ME!"
During courtship the male frigate bird (above) leans back on his tail, extends his wings, and with his beak pointing to the sky, inflates his deep red throat sac. He also claps his bill, making attractive rattling sounds.

THE EYES OF A FAN
The peacock's long tail, which is usually folded and stretched out behind him, opens into a splendid fan, designed to catch females' attention. The more eye motifs the tail contains, the more irresistible peahens will find him. The male also raises the crest on his head and makes his brightly colored breast feathers shimmer.

Mating

Courtship is successful when it leads to mating. To guarantee the survival of their species, animals must ensure that their sex cells (sperm and egg) come into contact with each other. Then fertilization and the **conception** of a new individual can take place. Fertilization takes place in a variety of ways. Internal fertilization is common among most land animals, including insects. External fertilization occurs among many aquatic animals.

FINDING A MATE BY SCENT
The male lion has a very sensitive nose. He can tell by sniffing the air carrying a lioness's scent when she is ready to mate. Lionesses in a pride usually are ready to mate at the same time, so that all the males can mate and no fighting occurs.

MATING SERENADE
Grasshopper males "sing" to attract a mate by rubbing their wings and legs together to produce a distinctive chirp. When a female comes along, the male climbs on her back, grips her sides, and fertilizes her eggs internally. The female then puts her ovipositor into the ground and lays her eggs. She covers them and leaves them to hatch.

■ MORE ABOUT DRAGONFLIES
Dragonflies are insects that have four large, veiny wings. There are about 5,000 species throughout the world, although most of them live in the Tropics. They are generally large, with wingspans of up to 6 inches (16 cm), and they are brightly colored. They have bulging **compound eyes** (eyes made up of thousands of individual lenses), often covering most of their heads. Dragonflies are predatory animals. While flying, they catch smaller insects with their legs. They can fly very fast and, because of their gracefulness and exceptional eyesight, have been known to catch and eat their own weight in food in just 30 minutes. Many species are territorial, patrolling an area and preventing other insects from entering or living there. After they mate, the females lay their eggs in water. Dragonfly larvae develop in the water, spending up to a year as nymphs. Then they climb up the stem of a reed, and finally emerge from their nymphal skins as adults.

MATING UNDERWATER
Both land tortoises and marine turtles achieve internal fertilization after a brief courtship consisting of head-bobbing, butting, and biting.

HEART-SHAPED MATING
During mating, dragonflies curve their bodies together into a heart shape as the male puts sperm into the female. They often fly together during mating and stay in this position until after the female has laid her eggs.

HERMAPHRODITES
Some invertebrates, including many species of worms, snails, and slugs, are **hermaphrodites**. This means that each individual has both male and female reproductive organs. During mating they act as both males and females, and both partners produce fertilized eggs.

Living in Groups

Many animals live in groups. There are random groups of animals, such as the gnu, which gather by the thousands during **migrations** in search of better pastures, and vultures, which flock together in food groups when they sight prey. Other groups are more highly organized. Fish move around in large schools, making it harder for a predator to pick out a single animal to catch. Birds move in flocks. It is easier for a whole flock to chase away a predator by attacking as a group, than it would be for a single bird. Some animals are even more highly organized. They live together in groups, and all the individuals in a group have specific roles and functions. They work together and cooperate for the good of the whole society.

FAMILIES IN THE DESERT
Slender-tailed meerkats live in the deserts of Southern Africa, in groups of 10 to 30 individuals, made up of several families. They shelter in a den together with ground squirrels and other species of meerkats. The families are closely knit, and the members help each other in everyday life. There is always an animal on guard, keeping one eye on the sky, to watch for birds of prey, and the other on the ground, to spot ground-level hunters. All members of the family help in the search for food and attack enemies that might threaten them.

A FEARSOME PACK
The wolf pack evolved as an effective way of capturing their prey—large herbivores that are often bigger than their hunters. Each wolf has a specific task to perform in hunting. Wolves usually assemble in large packs. In Italy, in areas where herbivores are scarce and the wolves have to make do with smaller prey, a pack may consist of only a few animals.

THE CAPE HUNTING DOG
Cape hunting dogs are related to wolves and dogs. They live south of the Sahara Desert, in the broad savanna of East and Southern Africa. Like wolves, Cape hunting dogs form quite large packs and hunt gnu, gazelles, and other antelope of the savanna. They can run for many miles chasing a gnu until the animal falls to the ground exhausted. As is the case with wolves, only one couple has pups. The others, which are often relatives of the dominant animal, do not reproduce, but help the mother raise her pups.

■ MORE ABOUT WOLVES

Until recently, wolves were some of the most widespread and most feared predators in temperate areas. They lived across North America from Alaska to Mexico, and also throughout northern Europe and Russia. The campaign to kill them off has reduced their numbers to a few thousand animals. In some places, however, their howls can still be heard. For example, in Yellowstone National Park, attempts are being made to reintroduce wolves. The wolf is a predator that feeds on almost any animal it can find in its territory, from small rodents to large herbivores, such as elk and deer, or even arctic musk oxen. Wolves' hunting strategies often vary according to the type of prey. Sometimes the pack roams the territory looking for field mice and rabbits. At other times long hunts for larger animals are organized. The territory of a wolf pack varies in size depending on the prey available and the number in the pack; more prey means a smaller territory. The packs communicate by howling.

Colonies

Some animals only come together at breeding time, forming extremely large colonies. The animals in the colony do not have specific tasks, and the groups break up soon after the reproduction period. Other animals form complex and highly organized structures, acting together almost as if they were a single individual. They live together throughout their lives.

HOME BUILDERS
Coral polyps are simple organisms. Each individual coral polyp is only a few millimeters long, but together the polyps build huge limestone structures that vary in shape according to the species (below left). Inside, the polyps, protected from external dangers, continue to enlarge their home. Some of these coral structures are incredibly old (perhaps more than a thousand years old). These tiny creatures have succeeded in building the largest biological structure on Earth, the Great Barrier Reef, in Australia.

DIVISION OF LABOR
The Portuguese man-of-war, related to jellyfish and coral, is not a single animal, but a group of small individuals called **zooids**. Each one of them has a precise function that it carries out as best it can. Some zooids have a "mouth," and they use their long tentacles to capture the little fish on which the colony feeds. Others are full of gas and keep the entire complex floating. The zooids that are responsible for reproduction produce sperm and eggs.

A HOST OF PENGUINS
During the long Antarctic winter, emperor penguins gather in the coldest zones of the South Pole for reproduction. There are about 30 huge colonies of these penguins, almost all on ice packs that remain stable throughout the winter. Just why they choose these sites, among the most inhospitable on Earth, may seem a mystery. In fact, the period when the young penguins need the greatest amounts of food for growth coincides with the beginning of the Antarctic spring. If they were to hatch at a milder time of year, they would need food most in the middle of winter, when their parents would not be able to find it.

A PROCESSION OF CATERPILLARS
Processionary caterpillars are best known for getting together in groups for finding food and defense. They spin large silk nests in the tops of pine trees. During the day they stay under cover in these shelters, where they are protected from predators. By night hundreds of caterpillars come out to look for food in long processions that can be over 30 feet (10 m) long. There is a group leader, and the others follow, one behind the other.

NESTS ON THE ROCKS
Boobies are among the most widespread marine birds. These elegant birds always make their nests in out-of-the-way sites, sometimes far from the mainland, such as on small islands off the coast. Here the birds gather in noisy colonies, where each pair builds a tiny nest. Despite the fact that they are so close to each other, the birds are quite aggressive and do not allow others in their territory, which is a few square inches around the nest. Marine birds are protected by living in colonies; it is hard for predators to attack such a large, aggressive group.

Flocking

Aggregations, or anonymous groups of animals, are the first stage in the development of animal societies. But aggregations do not happen by chance. While the individual animals may not know each other "personally," as is the case in mammalian societies, the huge groups of birds, insects, or fish have a precise defensive function. For example, very few predators succeed in penetrating the compact lines of a flock of birds. They can only do so if they can single out one bird. It is difficult to penetrate the flock, because the predator's sight is confused by so many wings in movement. An animal group can be formed for different reasons. The individual members seek each other either when food is needed or it is time to migrate. Other animals stay together in a group from birth. The success of these strategies is proven by the existence of schools of fish, flocks of birds, and migrating locusts.

THOUSANDS OF FINS
Many fish, especially vulnerable ones, such as these tropical jacks, form schools. Some fish, for example, sardines, remain in schools throughout their lives. They are often made up of millions of fish, and they swim in formation, followed by their predators, both human and animal. Aggregations of this type are anonymous groups, and the behavior of the animals is probably hereditary, even if the more sophisticated movements must be learned in the first stages of life.

A REAL CALAMITY
For the farmers of Southern Africa, the red-beaked quelea is a real problem. These small, perching birds appear in the fields without warning and can devastate crops. They assemble in flocks of thousands or of millions to forage for food, usually seeds. Predators have no chance of singling out one bird, and must wait until the flock stops to drink or nest. The trees on which they nest have to be enormous, for these small, sparrowlike birds build as many as 500 nests per tree.

■ MORE ABOUT LOCUSTS

Locusts belong to the order of insects called **Orthoptera** and are related to crickets and grasshoppers. The most important species is the desert locust, which lives in the areas around the Sahara Desert, and tends to move around in search of food. Sometimes vast swarms of locusts destroy the **crops** there as described in the Book of Exodus, in the Old Testament of the Bible.

The locust is a rather large insect, developing powerful wings in the adult phase. The rest of its body is also adapted for flight. For example, the intense activity of the muscles in flight forces air into the trachea (the insect's respiratory organs), so that more oxygen can be extracted and the insect can fly better. Under specific environmental conditions, a certain chemical substance makes the locusts mature more quickly so that the locust population can expand faster. The movements of locusts are not considered to be real migrations, because the individuals that leave first are not the same ones that come back to the place they left. Their lives are too short for them to return before dying.

MILLIONS OF HUNGRY MOUTHS

The migrations of locusts looking for food are well known. Only when food is scarce in the area do the larvae that hatch change into the migratory form of locusts, which then move in great masses. The other main form is the solitary, which generally moves alone. Migratory locusts congregate during the day in massive groups. They then migrate toward low-pressure areas, where they will find rain and new crops.

Societies

Social organization is the highest level of organization an animal species can achieve. Only a few species can be called truly social animals. Apart from humans, these include bees, ants, termites, and among mammals only chimpanzees and gorillas, and an African rodent that lives underground, called the naked mole rat. Other species instead form simpler organizations, which work just as well in coping with the problems posed by the environment as complex societies. The presence of insect societies in so many ecosystems shows how successful social organization is. Bees, ants, and termites have a rigidly structured society, in which the workers labor for the good of the colony without reproducing.

■ MORE ABOUT BEES

Of all the insects on Earth, those that are among the most successful are bees and ants. Bees belong to the order Hymenoptera. Bumblebee colonies, or societies, last for just one year, but the honeybee lives in permanent colonies. Since they "learned" how to live through the winter, bees have been able to create even larger colonies. "Ruled" by a queen, colonies may contain as many as 80,000 individuals. Unlike termites, honeybees do not divide tasks according to caste. All the worker bees participate in the work of the hive, changing jobs as they get older. The queen mates only once in her life with the males, or drones, which are then chased away by the workers.

ONLY EGGS FOR THE QUEEN
Termites, unlike bees and ants, belong to the Isoptera order. It is thought that the termite society developed so that a secretion vital to the survival of termites could be passed from one generation to the next. Since the generations live together for several years, a highly complex social life developed. Termites, like ants, are divided into **castes**: there are workers, soldiers, and a reproductive couple, the king and queen. The queen has an enormously enlarged abdomen and continuously produces eggs. In tropical countries termites dominate life on the savanna; they represent a large proportion of the animals in any given area, and they are able to alter the landscape by building mounds.

A SMALL COMMUNITY
When population density is high among rabbits, they dig a system of burrows in which about 20 adults live together. The dominant male and female live at the center of the colony, the place best protected from predators. The offspring of the dominant couple also tend to have a high social status, and therefore remain in the center of the colony. All the couples defend an area around their den, but there are also areas of common pasture. Those of lower rank live at the edge of the colony, where rabbit holes are difficult or even impossible to dig.

A SOCIETY OF WEAVERBIRDS
The social weaverbird is one of the most common birds in South Africa and Namibia. The weaverbird builds enormous nests, in which up to 300 birds can live. The nests are giant piles of grass and straw placed on trees, telephone poles, or platforms. Each couple builds a nest inside the mass of grass, and continues to bring fresh straw to it throughout the year. The birds shelter there at night and during the hottest part of the day. The nests of the sociable weaverbirds are also used by many other species, such as the African pygmy falcon and the gray acacia titmouse.

Cooperation

Some animals, such as sperm whales, will help other species when they are in danger, even if this means risking their lives. Other animals establish cooperative relationships with members of different species. If both species benefit from the relationship, it is called **symbiosis** (meaning "life together"). Animals mainly cooperate by keeping each other clean, providing food, or protecting one another from predators.

HELPING OUT

Sperm whales are protective of members of their group. If a whale is injured, the others gather around, their heads toward the middle, forming a circle known as the "daisy formation." This behavior is disastrous for the whales when they are being hunted, because it allows whalers to kill them off, one by one.

■ MORE ABOUT SPERM WHALES

The sperm whale has an enormous square head, taking up about one-third of its body length, and a small lower jaw. It lives in herds of 15 to 20 individuals. Female and juvenile whales live in temperate and tropical oceans throughout the world, while lone males also wander into colder polar waters. Males grow to about 60 feet (18 m) long; females are usually much smaller. Sperm whales are the largest of the toothed whales. They feed mainly on marine **mollusks** such as cuttlefish, squid, and octopus. Sperm whales dive deeper than any other aquatic mammal; they have been recorded at 3,900 feet (1,200 m) below the water's surface. They have been hunted extensively for waxy substances called spermaceti and ambergris, which are used to make cosmetics and ointments, and in perfume-making. Moby Dick, the most famous whale in literature and the main character in Herman Melville's novel, was a sperm whale.

The daisy formation

STICKING TOGETHER
Remoras, or shark suckers, have a sucker on the top of the head with which they attach themselves to sharks, turtles, or other large marine animals. The remoras do not harm their hosts. Instead they feed on small **parasites** on the shark's skin, helping to keep it clean. In return, the remoras are kept safe from predators and also get a banquet meal when the shark kills large prey.

CLEANING SERVICES IN EXCHANGE FOR FREE MEALS
Almost 2,500 years ago, the Ancient Greek historian Herodotus noticed that while all the other animals were afraid of the crocodile and kept a respectful distance from its gaping jaws, the tiny Egyptian plover roamed freely over its body and even fluttered about inside its huge mouth. He was the first to suggest that the bird was feeding on parasites on the reptile's skin and the remains of food left in its mouth. Modern naturalists have confirmed that this relationship is symbiotic. The plover also helps the crocodile by acting as a "watchdog," warning it of approaching danger by flying away.

DAIRY FARMER ANTS
Some ants protect herds of aphids from ladybugs. In return, the aphids provide them with honeydew, a nutritious sugary liquid the sap-sucking aphids produce. The ants "milk" the aphids by caressing them with their antennae.

Glossary

Adaptation An evolutionary change in a plant or animal that increases its ability to survive and reproduce in its environment.

Aggregation Flock or other collection of animals that group together to gather food, to mate, to migrate, or for some other common purpose.

Amphibian Member of the vertebrate class Amphibia, which lives both on land and in water. The class is divided into three main groups: those without tails; those with tails; and legless (caecilians).

Antenna One of a pair of feelers (antennae) on the head of many insects, crustaceans, and other invertebrates.

Aquatic Describes an animal or plant that grows or lives in or near water.

Asexual Describes an animal that reproduces without mating.

Baleen Plates of a material called keratin, which hang down from the upper jaw of toothless whales. The plates act like sieves to trap food from the water.

Brood Offspring produced at one hatching or birth.

Budding Method of asexual reproduction in simple organisms in which new individuals develop from outgrowths of cells (buds) on the parent.

Camouflage Means by which animals blend into their surroundings or otherwise deceive predators and escape their attention.

Carnivore Any meat-eating animal.

Carrion Dead flesh; carrion-eaters live on dead animals rather than killing live prey.

Caste A "social class" among some insects, such as termites. Different castes perform different tasks within the community.

Colony Group of animals that live close together. Colonial animals often consist of numerous individuals linked together.

Compound eyes Eyes of insects and some crustaceans that are made up of hundreds or even thousands of tiny lenses, each of which provides an image, giving the creature a wide area of vision.

Conception Moment of fusion of a female egg cell and a male sperm (fertilization) to form a new individual.

Crop Food storage compartment in the throat or stomach of birds and many invertebrates.

Crustacean Member of a group of hard-shelled, mainly aquatic animals, including crabs, shrimp, barnacles, and woodlice.

Dimorphism Occurrence of two forms in one species; sexual dimorphism is the difference between males and females.

Down Soft, fluffy feathers of young birds or the fine layer of feathers that forms the main insulation of adult birds.

Embryo 1. Young plant still enclosed in its seed. 2. Developing animal still in its egg or, in mammals, at an early stage of development inside the mother's body.

Evolution Process by which plants and animals change over successive generations. The result is often better adaptation to the environment and eventually, production of a new species.

Fertilization Joining of the sperm of a male animal and the egg of a female to produce a new individual.

Gastropod Member of a group of mollusks that includes snails and slugs. Most have a single, coiled shell with two pairs of head tentacles.

Gestation In animals that give birth to live young, the period of pregnancy from conception to birth.

Harem A group of animals consisting of one breeding male and several females, each with her own young.

Herbivore An animal that eats plants.

Hermaphrodite An animal or plant that has both male and female reproductive organs.

Hierarchy A "pecking order" in which social animals of higher status have the right, for example, to eat or mate ahead of ones of lower rank.

Incubation 1. Keeping eggs safe or warm until they hatch. 2. Period of time between laying and hatching of an egg.

Invertebrate Any animal without a backbone.

Larva (plural larvae) Stage in the metamorphosis of certain animals, such as butterflies and frogs. Caterpillars and tadpoles are larvae.

Lek Territory used by males for the sole purpose of attracting females.

Lepidoptera An order of insects that includes butterflies and moths.

Mammal Any member of the class Mammalia. All have at least some hair. The female feeds her young on milk from her body, and most give birth to active, live young.

Marsupials Mammals, such as kangaroos, which give birth to tiny young that continue to develop in a pouch on their mother's belly.

Matriarchy Group of female animals led by a dominant female. Males are allowed to enter the group only to mate.

Megapodes Ground-dwelling birds, including the mallee fowl, that rarely fly, and incubate their eggs in huge nests of rotting vegetation.

Metamorphosis Process in which some animals change their shape completely during their lifetime.

Migration Regular movement of animals from one area to another and back again at certain times of the year.

Mimicry When an animal, usually harmless, resembles another, usually harmful, animal and thereby gains protection from predators who fear to attack it.

Mollusks Any member of the phylum Mollusca; the name means soft, and most mollusks are soft-bodied, though many have shells. The group includes snails and slugs, octopuses and squid, and mussels.

Molt To shed feathers, hair, or skin.

Neonate Newborn animal.

Nymph Young of an insect, such as a grasshopper or a dragonfly, which resembles a small adult without wings.

Orthoptera The order of insects that includes grasshoppers and crickets.

Ovipositor Egg-laying tube of most female insects. In some, it is hidden; in others it sticks out from the hind end of the body.

Parasite Plant or animal that lives in or on another and feeds on it without benefiting its host.

Phonations Sounds that are too high- or low-pitched for humans, but which can be heard by whales.

Plankton Minute organisms that live on the surface of rivers, lakes, and oceans.

Pod Group of animals, such as seals and whales, that cooperate to catch food or protect their young.

Population density The number of plants or animals within a given area.

Preening Grooming behavior in birds that involves stroking their feathers to clean them, and sometimes spreading oil over them to make them waterproof.

Pupa (plural pupae) Stage in the metamorphosis of an insect between larva and adulthood. The pupa may move, but it cannot feed. The pupa of a butterfly or moth is called a chrysalis.

Regurgitate To bring up, for example, food stored in a bird's crop usually to feed its young.

Reptile Any member of the class Reptilia; vertebrates with scaly skin. They include snakes and lizards.

Symbiosis Close association between individuals of different species, from which both benefit.

Syrinx Vocal organ of a bird.

Veliger Free-swimming larva of many mollusks.

Vertebrate Animal with a backbone. Mammals, fish, birds, reptiles, and amphibians are all vertebrates.

Zooid An individual member of a colonial animal, such as a coral.

Index

Aggregations 54
Algae 11, 21
Amphibians 10, 11, 12, 32, 34, 40
Antlers 5, 28, 34
Ants 6, 56, 57
Aphids 59
Arabian oryx 9

Baboon 35, 39
Bacteria 5
Baleen 30
Bears 35
Bees 6, 56
Birds 10, 14, 15, 16, 20, 21, 22, 23, 32, 39, 45, 46, 50, 53, 54
Boobies 5, 53
Breeding 35, 41
Brood 17
Budding 9
Butterflies 12, 13

Camouflage 19
Cape hunting dogs 51
Carrion 29, 39, 46
Caterpillars 12, 13, 53
Cheetah 19, 25
Chicks 10, 15, 20, 23, 35, 46
Chimpanzee 19, 31, 56
Colonies 21, 34, 39, 52–53, 56, 57
Communication 30–31
Compound eyes 49
Conception 48

Cooperation 58, 59
Coral 8, 52
Courtship 18, 27, 28, 30, 40, 41, 46–47, 48, 49
Crocodile 7, 59
Cubs 19, 24, 35

Daisy formation 58
Darwin, Charles 6, 43
Deer 31, 34, 37, 44, 45
Down 10, 21

Eagles
  bald 46
  golden 23
Egret 34, 35
Elephant, African 5, 36
  Indian 23
Embryo 9, 10
  chicken 10
  frog 11, 12
  grasshopper 48
  Komodo dragon 29
Evolution 6

Fertilization 10, 40, 48, 49
Fiddler crab 43
Fish 15, 16, 21, 22, 34, 40, 42, 46, 54
Flamingos 20, 21
Frogs 10, 11, 16, 32, 42

Gastropods 10
Gazelles 51
  Thomson's 6

Gelada baboon 38, 39
Gestation 17, 19
Grasshoppers 32, 48, 55
Great-crested grebe 46, 47

Harems 31, 35, 36, 37, 39
Herbivores 11, 51
Hermaphrodites 49
Hierarchy 25, 28, 36, 38, 39, 45

Incubation 7, 8, 16
Insects 5, 12, 18, 20, 28, 32, 37, 48–49, 56

Larva 5, 8, 12, 20
Lek 44, 45
Lion 5, 34, 42, 48
Locusts 54, 55
Loners 40–41

Mammals 5, 6, 9, 10, 16, 18, 20, 22, 25, 27, 29, 32, 34, 37, 44
  aquatic, 21, 58
  egg-laying 16
  pouched 22
Mandibles 28
Mating 18, 20, 27, 28, 30, 32, 35, 40, 41, 43, 44, 48–49
  grounds 48–49
  season 16, 29, 36, 38, 41, 45
  underwater 49

Matriarchy 36
Metamorphosis 11, 12–13
Migrations 50, 55
Mollusks 58
Molt 9
Monkeys
  howler 42
  macaque 24
  society 16, 21, 34

Nests 7, 14–15, 17, 20, 21, 23, 35, 46, 53, 54, 57
Nymph, cicada 9
  dragonfly 49
  locust 55

Octopuses 41, 58
Orangutan 22
Ovipositor 12, 48

Phonations 30
Plankton 30
Population density 45
Pouch 17, 22, 24
Predators 5, 6, 14, 15, 18, 28, 36, 50, 51, 53, 54, 58
Pupa 12, 13, 20

Red-beaked quelea 54
Regurgitation 20
Reproduction 5, 8, 12
Reptiles 7, 10, 22, 59
Rivalry 28, 29
Ruff 45
Rut 31, 34, 37

Sage grouse 44, 45
Salamanders 32, 40
Sea horses 16, 17, 40
Sea lions 21, 37, 42
Seals 21, 42
Sexual dimorphism 26, 27, 28
Siamese fighting fish 27
Slug 10, 49
Snails 8, 10, 49
Sonograms 32
Sperm 8, 10, 40, 41, 48, 49, 52
Spider 18, 26, 27
Symbiosis 58

Tadpole 11, 12, 16
Termites 56, 57
Territory 29, 30, 33, 34, 35, 38, 42–43, 44, 45, 51, 53
Toads 14, 15, 32
Turtles 49, 59

Weaverbird 15, 57
Whales 21
  humpback 30–31
  sperm 58
Wings 12, 32, 39, 47, 49, 54, 55
Wolves 34, 35, 42, 51

Zebra 5, 38
Zooids 52

Further Reading

Brimner, Larry D. *Unusual Friendships: Symbiosis in the Animal World.*
    Franklin Watts, 1993.
Cherfas, Jeremy. *Animal Societies.* Lerner, 1991.
Fleisher, Paul. *Life Cycles of a Dozen Diverse Creatures.* Millbrook, 1996.
Taylor, Barbara. *Animal Homes.* Firefly, 1996.

Acknowledgments

The Publishers would like to thank the following photographers and archives for permission to reproduce pictures and for their assistance in providing pictures. The sources of the photographs are listed below. The following short forms have been used:

CAPPELLI = Giuliano Cappelli, Florence
CERFOLLI = Fulvio Cerfolli, Rome
JACANA = Jacana, Paris
NARDI = Marco Nardi, Florence
OKAPIA = Okapia, Frankfurt
OSF = Oxford Scientific Films, London
OVERSEAS = Overseas, Milan
PANDA = Panda Photo, Rome

1 Denis-Huot/BIOS–PANDA; 4 CAPPELLI; 5 C. Dani–I. Jeske; 6T-6B CERFOLLI; 7T N. J. Dennis/PANDA; 7C G. I. Bernard/OSF–OVERSEAS; 8T K. Bogon/WILDLIFE/PANDA; 8B P. Harrison/OSF–OVERSEAS; 9CL X. Eichaker/PANDA; 9CR CAPPELLI; 9B B. Cranston; 10T-10C CERFOLLI; 10B J. A .L. Cooke/OSF-OVERSEAS; 10BR P. Parks/OSF–OVERSEAS; 11T G. I. Bernard/OSF–OVERSEAS; 11C C. Nardin/JACANA-OVERSEAS; 13TL-13TC-13TR G. Cerchiari/PANDA; 13B R. Siniscalchi/PANDA; 14 H. D. Brandl/PANDA; 15T M. Fogden/OSF–OVERSEAS;15B D. Thompson/OSF–OVERSEAS; 17T N. J. Dennis/PANDA; 17C R. H. Kuiter/OSF–OVERSEAS; 17B J. Mallwitz/PANDA; 18 CAPPELLI; 19T N. J. Dennis/PANDA; 19B CAPPELLI; 20T J. A. L. Cooke/OSF–OVERSEAS; 20B CAPPELLI; 21 C. Grzimek/OKAPIA; 22T K. Wothe/OSF–OVERSEAS; 22B CAPPELLI; 23 E. Hanumantha Rad/PANDA; 25T Denis-Huot/BIOS–PANDA; 25C J. Hawkins/PANDA; 25B M. P. Pavese; 27T J. H. Robinson/OSF–OVERSEAS; 27C P. Varin/JACANA-OVERSEAS; 27B NARDI; 28T E. Coppola/PANDA; 28B C. Gaiasso/OVERSEAS; 29 CAPPELLI; 31T M.S. Terrace/OVERSEAS; 31C CAPPELLI; 31B CAPPELLI; 33T CAPPELLI; 33B Frederic/JACANA–OVERSEAS; 34 CAPPELLI; 35T Denis-Huot/BIOS–PANDA; 35B J. W. Warden/OVERSEAS; 36 Denis-Huot/BIOS–PANDA; 37T CAPPELLI; 37C J. C. Munoz/PANDA; 38 CAPPELLI; 39T ADN/PANDA; 39BR H. Eisenbeiss/PANDA; 39BL M. Gunther/PANDA; 40 S. Navarrini/PANDA; 41T S. Dimitrijevic/PANDA; 41C CAPPELLI; 42 CERFOLLI; 43 M. Fogden/OSF–OVERSEAS; 44T F. Mercay/PANDA; 44B A. Bardi/PANDA; 45T CAPPELLI; 45C D. C. Fritts/OVERSEAS; 45B F. Hazelhoff/PANDA; 47TR S. Cedola/PANDA; 47CL CAPPELLI; 47B CAPPELLI; 48T E. Dragesco/PANDA; 48B E. Coppola/PANDA; 49T Y. Lefevre/PANDA; 49B H. Ausloos/PANDA; 50 N. J. Dennis/PANDA; 51T CAPPELLI; 51B Denis-Huot/BIOS/PANDA; 52C P. Parks/OSF–OVERSEAS; 52B P. Petit/JACANA-OVERSEAS; 53T V. Bretagnolle/PANDA; 53C S. Resino/PANDA; 53B CAPPELLI; 54T B. Curtsinger/OVERSEAS; 54C-54B G. Cubitt/PANDA; 55 Y. Thonnerieux/PANDA; 56 CERFOLLI; 57T F. Winner /JACANA–OVERSEAS; 57C CAPPELLI; 57B A. Azzoni/OVERSEAS; 59T H. Ausloos/PANDA; 59C CAPPELLI; 59B R. Oggioni/PANDA